Oklahoma

Rich Smith

Visit us at
www.abdopublishing.com

Published by ABDO Publishing Company, 8000 West 78th Street, Suite 310, Edina, Minnesota 55439 USA. Copyright ©2010 by Abdo Consulting Group, Inc. International copyrights reserved in all countries. No part of this book may be reproduced in any form without written permission from the publisher. The Checkerboard Library™ is a trademark and logo of ABDO Publishing Company.

Printed in the United States.

Editor: John Hamilton
Graphic Design: Sue Hamilton
Cover Illustration: Neil Klinepier
Cover Photo: iStock Photo
Interior Photo Credits: AirPhoto-Jim Wark, Alamy, AP Images, City of Woodward, Corbis, Getty, Granger Collection, iStock Photo, John Hamilton, Jordan MacDonald, Jupiterimages, Library of Congress, Lin Harper, Mile High Maps, Mountain High Maps, North Wind Picture Archives, Oklahoma State University, One Mile Up, Peter Arnold Inc, PhotoResearchers, Tulsa 66ers, and the University of Oklahoma.
Statistics: State population statistics taken from 2008 U.S. Census Bureau estimates. City and town population statistics taken from July 1, 2007, U.S. Census Bureau estimates. Land and water area statistics taken from 2000 Census, U.S. Census Bureau.

Manufactured with paper containing at least 10% post-consumer waste

Library of Congress Cataloging-in-Publication Data

Smith, Rich, 1954-
  Oklahoma / Rich Smith.
    p. cm. -- (The United States)
  Includes index.
  ISBN 978-1-60453-671-3
  1. Oklahoma--Juvenile literature. I. Title.

  F694.3.S64 2010
  976.6--dc22

                        2008052394

Table of Contents

The Sooner State...4

Quick Facts 6

Geography 8

Climate and Weather 12

Plants and Animals..14

History..18

Did You Know?...24

People...26

Cities 30

Transportation..34

Natural Resources 36

Industry...38

Sports 40

Entertainment..42

Timeline...44

Glossary...46

Index..48

The Sooner State

Oklahoma is in the Great Plains region of the south-central United States. It is a beautiful place of grassy ranges, sparkling rivers, lush forests, low hills, and modern cities. Also, Oklahoma is a place where many vital kinds of business are located. It is one of America's most important oil producing states.

Oklahoma's nickname comes from the word for people who sneaked into the territory ahead of everyone else. Oklahoma was opened to settlers in events known as "land runs." Settlers weren't supposed to claim their land until a specific date. Those who couldn't wait went in sooner. So, they became known as "sooners." They call Oklahoma the Sooner State in honor of all who just can't wait to enjoy all the good things that Oklahoma offers.

Oklahoma's capitol features
a bronze sculpture called
As Long as the Waters Flow.
It is a reminder of a treaty created
between Native Americans and
the U.S. government that said
tribes would own their lands as
long as the grass grows and the
rivers run.

Quick Facts

OKLAHOMA

Name: Oklahoma is a Native American Choctaw word that means "land of the red people."

State Capital: Oklahoma City

Date of Statehood: November 16, 1907 (46th state)

Population: 3,642,361 (28th-most populous state)

Area (Total Land and Water): 69,898 square miles (181,035 sq km), 20th-largest state

Largest City: Oklahoma City, population 547,274

Nickname: The Sooner State

Motto: *Labor omnia vincit* (Labor conquers all things)

State Bird: Scissor-Tailed Flycatcher

State Flower: Mistletoe

State Rock: Barite Rose

State Tree: Redbud

State Song: "Oklahoma!"

Highest Point: 4,973 feet (1,516 m), Black Mesa

Lowest Point: 289 feet (88 m), Little River

Average July Temperature: 82°F (28°C)

Record High Temperature: 120°F (49°C) in Tipton, June 27, 1994

Average January Temperature: 37°F (3°C)

Record Low Temperature: -27°F (-33°C) in Watts, January 18, 1930

Average Annual Precipitation: 34 inches (86 cm)

Number of U.S. Senators: 2

Number of U.S. Representatives: 5

U.S. Postal Service Abbreviation: OK

Black Mesa

Low Point: Little River

Geography

Oklahoma is in the south-central United States. Its neighbor to the north is Kansas. To the east are Missouri and Arkansas. South and west of Oklahoma is Texas. Oklahoma's other western neighbors are New Mexico and Colorado.

Oklahoma is shaped like a frying pan. The handle is on the west side of the state. It is called the Panhandle region. The pot-shaped part is the eastern half. Oklahoma covers 69,898 square miles (181,035 sq km). It is the 20th-largest state.

Oklahoma's highest point is a long summit called Black Mesa. It rises 4,973 feet (1,516 m) above sea level. It is located in the northwestern corner of the state.

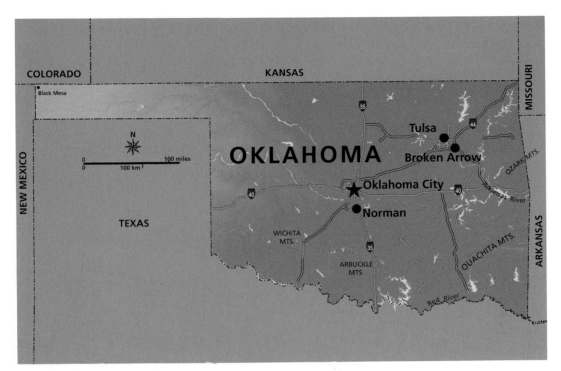

Oklahoma's total land and water area is 69,898 square miles (181,035 sq km). It is the 20th-largest state. The state capital is Oklahoma City.

All of Oklahoma is one very long slope, which becomes lower the farther east you travel from Black Mesa. The lowest point is along the Little River in the southeast. It is just 289 feet (88 m) above sea level.

Oklahoma has six natural regions. The farthest west is the mostly open plains of the Panhandle region. Next to it are the prairie lands of the Central Plateau. To the east of the Central Plateau is the lightly wooded Arkansas Valley. To the south is the Red River Valley. The tree-covered Ozark Mountain region is in the northeast corner. The Ouachita Mountain region is directly south of the Ozarks.

Oklahoma's four main ranges are the Ozark, Ouachita, Arbuckle and Wichita Mountains. Its most important rivers are the Arkansas and Red Rivers.

The Red River.

Mt. Scott in the Wichita Mountain Range is one of Oklahoma's tallest mountains, rising 2,464 feet (751 m) above sea level. It is a legendary site. Tales of ancient spirits, Spanish gold, and buried outlaw loot bring curious visitors to the mountain each year.

Climate and Weather

Oklahoma has a continental type of climate. That means cold in the winter and hot in the summer. In January, the average temperature is about 37° Fahrenheit (3°C). In July, the average temperature is close to 82° Fahrenheit (28°C).

Southeast Oklahoma is the rainiest part of the state. More than 50 inches (127 cm) of precipitation fall there each year. It's humid

Lightning strikes during a storm in central Oklahoma.

because of moist winds blowing inland from the Gulf of Mexico. The driest part of the state is the Panhandle, which is too far for Gulf of Mexico moisture to reach. Its annual average rainfall is just 15 inches (38 cm).

Oklahoma is in the middle of a severe weather zone called Tornado Alley. More big tornados occur in Oklahoma than almost anywhere else. About 52 twisters touch ground in a typical year.

A violent tornado sweeps across northwest Oklahoma, near the town of Arnett. This tornado was part of a tornado outbreak on May 4, 2007, that killed more than 12 people.

Plants and Animals

Three-quarters of Oklahoma is covered by prairie grass. The most common grasses are buffalo, bluestem, grama, and sand lovegrass. These prairie grasses obtain some of the water they need from the many streams and creeks that flow through the state. Along these brooks grow dry-climate trees, such as junipers, pinyon pines, and ponderosa pines.

Cactus is found in the Black Mesa portion of the Panhandle. The state's official flower is mistletoe.

Most Oklahoma forests are in the rainy southeastern part of the state. Trees include shortleaf pine, loblolly pine, and cypress. The northeastern corner of the state is home to forests of cedar, elm, and oak.

Orange butterfly milkweed blooms in Tall Grass Prairie, Oklahoma.

Black bears live in the eastern forests of Oklahoma. Also found are red and gray foxes, bobcats, badgers, and white-tailed deer. The white-tailed deer live just about everywhere in Oklahoma. Pronghorn antelope are seen mainly in the Panhandle.

Long ago, vast herds of bison roamed the state. Today, only a few small herds remain. The same is true of elk. However, Oklahoma has large numbers of prairie dog colonies. It also has many armadillos.

Perched on tree branches and darting across the skies of Oklahoma are birds such as the bald eagle, red-tailed hawk, cardinal, and woodpecker. There also are pheasant, quail, and greater prairie chickens.

There are many snakes and reptiles in Oklahoma. The collared lizard is the Oklahoma state reptile.

Splashing around in the state's lakes and rivers are catfish, bass, sunfish, and crappie.

A bison walks past a black-tailed prairie dog in Comanche County.

Armadillo

Collared Lizard

Pronghorn

History

Not many Native Americans lived in Oklahoma before the coming of explorers from Europe. Mostly, tribes just wandered through Oklahoma on their way to someplace else. Indians first began

Spanish explorers arrived in Oklahoma in the 1540s.

staying permanently in Oklahoma about 700 years before the arrival of explorer Francisco Vásquez de Coronado and the Spanish conquistadors in the 1540s.

Men from Spain were followed 140 years later by French explorers. They claimed for France all the lands of the Mississippi River basin, including Oklahoma. In 1796, the French built their first permanent community in Oklahoma.

In 1803, Oklahoma came under the control of the United States. It was bought from France as part of the famous Louisiana Purchase.

At first, Oklahoma was known as Indian Territory. It became known as Oklahoma in 1866, when the chief of the Choctaw Indians suggested the United States call it that. Oklahoma in the Choctaw language means "land of the red people."

Oklahoma was first known as Indian Territory. The Choctaw word *Oklahoma* means "land of the red people."

Oklahoma was a place where the United States government sent Native Americans it no longer welcomed. The land was for Indians only. The most important of the tribes brought to Oklahoma were the Choctaw, Cherokee, Seminole, Creek, and Chickasaw. They are called the Five Civilized Tribes.

In the late 1870s, pioneers began demanding that the government allow whites to settle in Oklahoma. The United States opened a small section of Oklahoma for the settlers. The government also agreed to give the land away to anyone who wanted it. About 50,000 people who wanted Oklahoma land lined up along the border on the morning of April 22, 1889. A whistle blew, and then people raced into Oklahoma to pick out the land they wanted. More of these "land runs" took place over the years that followed, until most of Oklahoma was in the hands of settlers. In 1907, Oklahoma officially became a state.

Homesteaders rush to stake their claims in Oklahoma.

In the early 1900s, oil was discovered in Oklahoma. Many people became wealthy almost overnight. The city of Tulsa quickly changed from a sleepy town to a busy city.

An oil well in Oklahoma in 1922. When oil was discovered, many people became rich overnight.

A dust storm blasts an Oklahoma farm family in 1936.

But hard times fell on Oklahoma in the early 1930s. America's economy collapsed during the Great Depression. Also, for a long time the rains stopped coming. Wheat crops failed. Cattle starved. Strong winds blew dirt everywhere. Oklahoma became known as part of the Dust Bowl. Many people moved away.

After World War II, prosperity returned to Oklahoma. The rains came back and the crops grew. In recent years, the state has also diversified its economy. It tries to attract other kinds of businesses and rely less on agriculture. Oklahoma today is a good state in which to live, work, play, and learn.

Did You Know?

Oklahoma City, OK

Indianapolis, IN

- One of the Top 10 all-time deadliest tornados struck in Oklahoma in 1947. More than 180 people were killed and 970 injured.

- There are only two capital cities in the United States named after their state. Oklahoma City is one of them. Indianapolis, Indiana, is the other.

- More than half of all the people in Oklahoma live in or near the state's two biggest cities, Oklahoma City and Tulsa.

- America's most famous historical highway was Route 66. It was featured in the 2006 animated film *Cars*. Route 66 stretched from Chicago, Illinois, to Los Angeles, California, and passed through Oklahoma. Route 66 was dreamed up by Tulsa businessman Cyrus Avery in the 1920s.

- Catoosa, Oklahoma, is home to an 80-foot (24-m) -long, concrete Blue Whale. The popular attraction was built along Route 66 by Hugh Davis in the early 1970s as an anniversary gift to his wife Zelta, who collected whale figurines.

People

Ron Howard (1954-) is one of Hollywood's most famous celebrities. His best-known early role was in television's *The Andy Griffith Show.* He played little Opie Taylor. He grew up and played Richie Cunningham on the comedy show *Happy*

Days. Later, he became a movie director. Some of his films include *Splash*, *Backdraft*, *Apollo 13*, and *How the Grinch Stole Christmas.* Howard was born in Duncan.

Will Rogers (1879-1935) made America laugh during the Great Depression of the 1930s. He told funny stories and twirled a rope lasso while he told them. His lasso tricks were so good that he made it into *The Guinness Book of World Records.* He also appeared in many movies, and wrote an opinion column that ran in 4,000 newspapers. Rogers was born near Oologah.

Carl Albert (1908-2000) was an Oklahoma member of Congress who served as speaker of the House of Representatives from 1971 until 1977. The speaker is the most powerful person in Washington after the president and vice president. Albert was born in McAlester.

Charles "Pretty Boy" Floyd (1904-1934) was one of America's most notorious bank robbers. He was on the FBI's Ten Most Wanted Fugitives list. Floyd was caught by police after many stickups, but escaped on his way to prison. He then robbed even more banks. Finally, Floyd died in a shoot-out with law officers. He was born in Georgia, but was raised in Oklahoma's Cookson Hills.

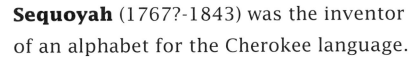

Sequoyah (1767?-1843) was the inventor of an alphabet for the Cherokee language. His alphabet made it possible for other members of his tribe to share ideas and information in writing. Being able to read and write helped the Cherokees do many great things. Sequoyah was active in Cherokee tribal politics after moving to Oklahoma in 1828.

Johnny Bench (1947-) was one of the greatest catchers in baseball history. He played for the Cincinnati Reds from 1967 until 1983. He helped his team win the World Series in 1975 and again in 1976. Bench was born in Oklahoma City.

Cities

Oklahoma City is the state capital. It is also Oklahoma's biggest city. It has a population of 547,274. The city was founded in 1889. The 607 square miles (1,572 sq km) it covers make Oklahoma City one of the nation's most sprawling cities. The economy of Oklahoma City until the 1980s was mainly dependent on the oil industry. Today, its economy is much more diverse. It now includes healthcare, biotechnology, and information technology.

Tulsa in 1909.

Tulsa was once known as the Oil Capital of the World.

Tulsa is Oklahoma's second-largest city. Its population is about 384,037. Tulsa was settled by the Creek Native American tribe in the 1830s. Tulsa once was known as the Oil Capital of the World. The oil industry is still important to the city's economy. But now, so are aerospace, technology, finance, and telecommunications.

Branched lightning strikes near the Norman, Oklahoma, Doppler radar installation (round-roofed building).

Oklahoma's third-largest city is **Norman,** with a population of about 106,707. Norman is just a few miles south of Oklahoma City. The National Weather Service has its Storm Prediction Center and Severe Storms Laboratory in Norman. The city is also home to several important companies that make high-tech products and medicines.

Broken Arrow is a suburb of Tulsa. Its population is about 90,714. It is a city filled with businesses, such as Blue Bell Creameries and Advanced Medical Instruments. Only two other Oklahoma cities have as many companies as Broken Arrow.

An early farm family statue and Main Street in Broken, Arrow, Oklahoma.

Transportation

The city of Catoosa, near Tulsa, is the home of the farthest inland river port in America. Barges filled with Oklahoma farm products and manufactured goods leave the port and travel along the Arkansas River and then the Mississippi River. The barges end their journey at seaports in Louisiana.

The Arkansas River runs through Tulsa, Oklahoma.

Also along this same waterway is Oklahoma's other river port, the Port of Muskogee.

There are more than 150 public airports in Oklahoma. The largest is Will Rogers World Airport in Oklahoma City. The second largest is Tulsa International Airport. But the busiest is Tulsa's Riverside-Jones Airport.

Only one regional passenger train serves Oklahoma. It is the Amtrak Heartland Flyer, which travels between Oklahoma City and Fort Worth, Texas.

An open road in Oklahoma.

The state has more than 12,000 miles (19,312 km) of highways, turnpikes, and toll roads.

Natural Resources

Slightly more than three-quarters of Oklahoma land is used for agriculture. Much of that is set aside for cattle ranching. Wheat is Oklahoma's most important farm crop.

Oklahoma is famous for its cattle. The Wichita Mountains Wildlife Refuge keeps a herd of Texas longhorn cattle. Introduced in the 1500s by Spanish explorers, by the 1920s longhorns were nearly extinct. Today, there are enough longhorns that some are sold to ranchers each year.

Wheat is harvested on a farm outside of Walters, Oklahoma.

Oklahoma contains the nation's fifth-largest supply of crude oil waiting to be pumped out of the

A pumpjack helps lift the oil out of the ground.

ground. Natural gas is often found when drilling for oil. Oklahoma is America's second-greatest producer of natural gas.

Forestry is a small but important part of the Oklahoma economy. Forests cover about 17 percent of the state. Nearly two-thirds of Oklahoma forests are used in the production of lumber, paper, and other goods.

Industry

The biggest employer in Oklahoma is the government. In 2007, there were nearly as many Oklahomans working for federal, state, and local governments as there were living in all of Tulsa. The next biggest employer in Oklahoma is the transportation industry. There are also a great many schoolteachers and university professors.

Businesses making the most money for Oklahoma are in the services sector. These include banks, financial companies, insurance firms, law firms, accounting agencies, and companies that provide information.

The biggest employer in Oklahoma is the government.

Aerospace is sky-high in terms of importance to Oklahoma. A number of companies in Tulsa help make engines that propel jets and rockets. Tulsa also has the world's largest maintenance facility for jetliners.

Manufacturing is another important part of Oklahoma's economy. Products made in Oklahoma include tires, equipment for the oil industry, and air conditioners.

A repairman works on a damaged jet plane's tail section. Tulsa, Oklahoma, has the world's largest maintenance facility for jetliners.

Sports

The Oklahoma City Thunder is a National Basketball Association team. Oklahoma is also home to the Tulsa 66ers, a minor-league basketball team. The state also has minor-league football, baseball, hockey, and soccer teams.

Many people enjoy watching college football in Oklahoma. The state's two big schools are the University of Oklahoma and Oklahoma State University. They are regularly ranked by sports writers as among the nation's best for football and many other sports.

Popular recreational sports and activities in Oklahoma include fishing and boating, golfing, and rodeo. Spread across Oklahoma are 45 state parks and recreation areas, plus one national recreation area. There also are 140,696 acres (56,938 hectares) of national reserves where wildlife can be viewed.

A steer wrestler competes in the Woodward Elks Rodeo in Woodward, Oklahoma. Annual festivals and rodeos have been part of Oklahoma's history for as long as most can remember.

Entertainment

Famous actor groups, ballet troupes, choirs, and symphony orchestras are all found in Oklahoma. One of America's most beloved musical productions is called *Oklahoma!* Its official home today is the outdoor amphitheater in Sand Springs, about 10 miles (16 km) south of Tulsa. The musical is presented dozens of times each summer. It stars a frequently changing cast of well-known entertainers.

Many fine libraries and museums exist in Oklahoma. One of the best for learning about Native American life is the Five Civilized Tribes Museum in Muskogee.

State fairs are held in Tulsa and Oklahoma City each September. Both offer thrill rides, exhibits, and contests. Many people also like watching the colorful and exciting powwows put on by Native Americans throughout the year.

In Anadarko, Oklahoma, the Kiowa Black Leggings Ritual Powwow is one of the Kiowa people's most important events. It honors people who served in the military.

Timeline

1540s—Spanish conquistadors explore western Oklahoma.

1682—France claims Oklahoma.

1803—The U.S. buys the Louisiana Territory from France, which includes most of present-day Oklahoma.

1830-1842—Native Americans from the southeastern U.S. are forced to move into Oklahoma by the federal government.

1889—Federal government opens Oklahoma to white settlers. First of several "land runs" is held.

OKLAHOMA

1907—Oklahoma becomes the 46th state in the Union.

1930s—Drought strikes Oklahoma. It becomes known as the Dust Bowl. Thousands of people take what they have left and leave the state.

1940s—World War II and post-war economic boom put Oklahoma back on its feet.

1995—A terrorist bomb strikes the Alfred P. Murrah Federal Building in Oklahoma City, killing 168 people.

2003—University of Oklahoma quarterback Jason White wins the Heisman Trophy.

Glossary

Bison—A large, four-legged mammal with a humped back. Its front is huge and covered with shaggy fur. It is improperly called a buffalo.

Conquistadors—Spanish soldiers and explorers who came to the New World in the 1500s and used force to conquer native people and take control of their lands.

Dust Bowl—An area in the 1930s that included parts of Oklahoma, Kansas, and north Texas. Severe drought and soil erosion caused crops to fail, forcing many people to move away.

Great Plains—The land east of the Rocky Mountains, west of the Mississippi River and stretching from Canada to the Mexican Border. It is mostly covered with grass and few trees.

Louisiana Purchase—A large area of land in North America purchased from France in 1803. The land went from the Mississippi River to the Rocky Mountains and from the Gulf of Mexico to the Canadian border. This land was later split into 15 new states, including Oklahoma.

Powwow—In modern times, a gathering of American Indians who honor their past with traditional music, singing, and dancing while wearing ceremonial clothing. Powwows can last for several hours or several days.

Tornado—A violent windstorm. Its main feature is a dark, funnel-shaped cloud that reaches down to the ground. The funnel cloud destroys almost everything in its path.

Tornado Alley—An area of the United States that has many tornadoes. Tornado Alley stretches from Texas in the south to North Dakota in the north and east to parts of Ohio.

Waterway—A stream or river wide and deep enough for boats to travel along.

Index

A
Advanced Medical
    Instruments 33
Albert, Carl 28
America (*See* United
    States)
Amtrak Heartland
    Flyer 35
Andy Griffith Show,
    The 26
Apollo 13 26
Arbuckle Mountains 10
Arkansas 8
Arkansas River 10, 34
Arkansas Valley 10
Avery, Cyrus 25

B
Backdraft 26
Bench, Johnny 29
Black Mesa 8, 10, 14
Blue Bell Creameries
    33
Blue Whale 25
Broken Arrow, OK 33

C
Cars 25
Catoosa, OK 25, 34
Central Plateau 10
Cherokee (tribe) 20,
    29
Chicago, IL 25
Chickasaw (tribe) 20
Choctaw (tribe) 19, 20
Cincinnati Reds 29
Colorado 8
Congress, U.S. 28
Cookson Hills 28
Coronado, Francisco
    Vásquez de 18
Creek (tribe) 20, 31
Cunningham, Richie
    26

D
Davis, Hugh 25
Davis, Zelta 25
Duncan, OK 26
Dust Bowl 23

E
Europe 18

F
FBI 28
Five Civilized Tribes
    20
Five Civilized Tribes
    Museum 43
Floyd, Charles "Pretty
    Boy" 28
Fort Worth, TX 35
France 18, 19

G
Georgia 28
Great Depression 23,
    27
Great Plains 4
Guinness Book of
    World Records, The
    27
Gulf of Mexico 12

H
Happy Days 26
Hollywood, CA 26
House of
    Representatives 28
How the Grinch Stole
    Christmas 26
Howard, Ron 26

I
Indian Territory 19
Indianapolis, IN 24

K
Kansas 8

L
Little River 10
Los Angeles, CA 25
Louisiana 34
Louisiana Purchase 19

M
McAlester, OK 28
Mississippi River 18,
    34
Missouri 8
Muskogee, OK 43

N
National Basketball
    Association 40
National Weather
    Service 32
New Mexico 8
Norman, OK 32

O
Oklahoma! 42
Oklahoma City, OK 24,
    29, 30, 32, 35, 43
Oklahoma City
    Thunder 40
Oklahoma State
    University 40
Oologah, OK 27
Ouachita Mountain
    region 10
Ouachita Mountains
    10
Ozark Mountain
    region 10
Ozark Mountains 10

P
Panhandle region 8,
    10, 12, 14, 16
Port of Muskogee 35

R
Red River 10

Red River Valley 10
Riverside-Jones
    Airport 35
Rogers, Will 27
Route 66 25

S
Sallisaw, OK 29
Sand Springs, OK 42
Seminole (tribe) 20
Sequoyah 29
Severe Storms
    Laboratory 32
Spain 18
Splash 26
Storm Prediction
    Center 32

T
Taylor, Opie 26
Texas 8, 35
Tornado Alley 13
Tulsa, OK 22, 24, 25,
    31, 33, 34, 38, 39,
    42, 43
Tulsa International
    Airport 35
Tulsa 66ers 40

U
United States 4, 8, 19,
    20, 23, 24, 27, 28,
    34, 37, 42
University of
    Oklahoma 40

W
Washington, D.C. 28
Wichita Mountains 10
Will Rogers World
    Airport 35
World Series 29
World War II 23